TRAP

A Play for I

NAM

SAMUEL FRENCH

LONDON
NEW YORK TORONTO SYDNEY HOLLYWOOD

CHARACTERS

(in order of their appearance)

JOVANKA, an old cleaning woman
A FEMALE PRISON GUARD
SECTION OFFICER GRETA JANEK
ASSISTANT PRISON SUPERINTENDENT ANNA KRISNOV
LOUISE DELANEY, an American "exchange" teacher
DORA BYERS, an English assistant headmistress
MARY VICKERS, an English headmistress
EMMA HIPP, a German teacher who has been working in England
JANE WALTERS, an infants teacher

The action takes place in the historic fortress prison of Cistomek, in a country in Central Europe

Time—the middle sixties of the twentieth century

TRAP

SCENE—*A prison cell.*

The cell is a broad one, built of stone, and of very ancient origin, though it has been to some extent modernized. A broad iron grille runs the entire length of the back wall. In this there is a full-sized grille door, behind which is a passage, stone backed and lit by a thick guarded light. The passage exits R. *Down* L *is a thinner door of much later construction than the rest of the place. Running up stage from this to the back grille is a wooden seat or bench. Another seat runs the length of the* R *wall, and this is fixed to the stonework with metal supports. Low in the wall, and far down* R *is a metal grille about six to nine inches. Throughout the action there is a constant background of feet walking on stone floors, clashing of grilles and heavy doors. A voice, distorted through a Tannoy, makes requests for certain prison officers and sometimes issues a general order. Infrequently there is a burst of heavy march music.*

When the CURTAIN *rises, a table and two chairs are stacked against the* R *wall.* JOVANKA, *an old harridan of a cleaning woman, is sweeping the place with a total lack of enthusiasm. She smokes, keeping the cigarette in her mouth and blowing past it, squinting through the fumes. She finishes sweeping and places the table* C, *with a chair on either side. Then she sweeps under the seats with a brush and pan, smoking and coughing. A* WOMAN GUARD, *with blue military-style jacket, plain peaked cap, full skirt and jackboots, and carrying a slung submachine-gun, comes to the open grille and surveys* JOVANKA, *who moves* L *of the door down* L, *opens it, and is about to go in with the mop and bucket.*

GUARD. You've not much time.

JOVANKA (*truculently*) I get enough orders without *you* chippin' in!

(*The* GUARD *chuckles, as if implying Jovanka is a hard case*)

Get on with your guarding!

(*The* GUARD, *still grinning, turns and strolls out through the grille and off* R. JOVANKA *exits into the lavatory* L, *mops perfunctorily and flushes the pan. While she is doing this the loudspeaker voice is heard—a female voice*)

LOUDSPEAKER VOICE (*off; distorted*) Section Officer Janek will inspect cell number ten, floor D. Section Officer Janek will inspect cell number ten, floor D.

JOVANKA (*with a croaking chuckle*) That's right, me sprightly young section officer. Come and find fault! (*She coughs, hawks and spits. Then, realizing what she has done, she wipes the floor where she spat, straightens and salutes ironically*) Long live the Republic!

(SECTION OFFICER GRETA JANEK *enters through the open grille door, observing Jovanka's performance as she comes in. She is in her mid-twenties, slim, dark and classically beautiful, with her hair drawn severely under her military cap. Her uniform has a military jacket and fully cut skirt, all dark blue, and she wears low heeled jackboots. Across each red epaulette is a thin gold stripe. Her voice is pleasant, well controlled. In her job, she has to learn to be unemotional. She carries a bunch of keys*)

GRETA. And what's got into you, Comrade Cleaner Jovanka?

JOVANKA. I just thought . . .

GRETA. No saluting is required of you, and not much thought, either. (*She draws a finger along the seat* R *and looks accusingly at the cleaner*) But cleaning *is* required! What about that?

JOVANKA (*moving to Greta and peering*) Me eyes is bad. What about what?

GRETA. Dust!

JOVANKA. Can't see it. No spectacles. Been waiting for 'em far too long as it is.

GRETA. Don't imply criticism of the state medical

service. Just use a duster where you'd expect to find dust. (*She picks up a duster from the bench and throws it at Jovanka*) Here.

(JOVANKA *catches the duster and stares at it owlishly*)

(*Edgily*) Dust, I said! There isn't much time.

(JOVANKA *starts dusting* R. GRETA *crosses to the door down* L *and looks inside*)

JOVANKA. I cleaned in *there*.
GRETA. Naturally.

(ASSISTANT PRISON SUPERINTENDENT ANNA KRISNOV *appears along the passage and enters, coming down* C *to the table. She is in her mid-forties, ruthlessly efficient, but there is no sadism in her. She is dressed similarly to the Section officer but her cap peak has a gold band round it, and her epaulettes bear two broad gold stripes*)

ANNA. Section Officer Janek.

(GRETA *turns and salutes.* ANNA *returns the salute formally, then rounds on the motionless and staring Jovanka*)

What are you staring at, woman?
JOVANKA. I ain't staring . . .
ANNA. Madam! Address me properly, woman! Have you finished in here?
JOVANKA. Yes—madam.

(ANNA *looks enquiringly at* GRETA, *who nods*)

ANNA (*to the cleaner*) Out.

(JOVANKA, *still with cigarette in mouth, looks as sullen as she dare, and starts to pick up her clobber, muttering*)

JOVANKA. I dunno. Some people seem to think you're a bloody machine. Just a machine. Don't achieve no norms or targets just sweeping up. All yer get is the same stuff to do all over again . . .

(ANNA *steps forward, whips the disgusting fag-end out of Jovanka's mouth and throws it into her bucket.* JOVANKA *does not dare raise her voice in protest*)

ANNA. Filthy habit!

JOVANKA. Huh! Government sells the tobacco, don't it?

ANNA. Out!

(ANNA, *having given the order, dismisses Jovanka from her mind and takes a walk of inspection around the cell, allowing* JOVANKA *time to get through the grille door and into the passage. While Anna's back is turned,* JOVANKA *retrieves the fag-end from her bucket, puts it in her mouth, makes a face, then shuffles off.* GRETA *sees this, and a momentary pucker of humour lights up her reposeful face. The echoing noises off, the walking and the occasional doors, continue.* GRETA *locks the lavatory door, turning as* ANNA *crosses to her down* L. ANNA *is less formal now; she is friendly, and a little concerned for Greta*)

Everything all right?

GRETA. I think so.

ANNA (*moving to the door and rapping on it*) Locked.

GRETA. You did say that I was to be in charge.

ANNA. Yes.

GRETA. I took you at your word, ma'am.

(*The wall phone, up* L, *gives a series of high-pitched buzzes*)

ANNA (*lifting the phone*) Assistant Superintendent Krisnov. Yes? (*She turns and faces Greta with a warning face and mouths the name "Mischek", then turns abruptly and stands rigid, answering correctly and dutifully. As she speaks, she turns gradually so that the audience can see she is controlling her temper, her real feelings being revealed by her expression while her voice remains studiously controlled*) Yes, sir. Speaking . . . Yes, sir, she *will* be in charge . . . (*She beckons to Greta*)

(GRETA *tiptoes over to* R *of Anna and listens close so as to catch the words at the earpiece*)

I thought I made myself clear, sir. Janek is ideally suited for this work. She has a highly retentive memory for files and data, she is objective, she is fair-minded and extremely tenacious . . .

(*They listen to the Superintendent expressing doubts and warnings. They exchange glances.* ANNA *looks grim, and explains mildly and carefully*)

Yes, sir . . . Yes . . . I *do* regard her as my responsibility . . . Yes . . . Good-bye, sir. (*She replaces the receiver, staring at Greta*)

GRETA. I'm not popular with Superintendent Mischek.

ANNA. A mistake would please him *greatly.*

GRETA. What would he do?

ANNA (*unable to keep on her mask of indifference*) He'd—probably have my rank and my pension.

GREAT. What?

ANNA. He's got Bragodine all lined up for prison superintendent's job. He knows I'm in the running for another gold bar. A *woman* superintendent! He hates the idea.

GRETA. If you think I ought to step down . . .

ANNA. And me climb down to *him?* (*Moving close to Greta*) Just prove I'm right about you.

GRETA. I will.

ANNA. You are just the sort of person we want. Look at me: when the Germans were here, I was nineteen.

GRETA. And I was a month or so old.

ANNA. You're a good advertisement for what the state can do, Greta. At least, we took care of the children.

GRETA. And I hope I've given service, in return.

ANNA. And another thing—with a father buried in a partisan's grave in the mountains, and a mother who— I mean, you're not the sort to look over your shoulder, too much.

GRETA. True.

ANNA (*taking out a notebook*) We haven't any dossiers available on any of them. Not under these names, at least. But if that computer brain of yours hits on anything, good luck to you. Now—all five of them say that they're teachers. Miss Mary Vickers, fifty-two, English. Miss Dora Byers, forty-two, English. Fraulein Emma Hipp, German . . .

GRETA. *West* German. Working in England, though.

ANNA. She's intelligent, and tough. Oh! (*She remembers, and moves down* R) The gas vent—has it been checked? (*She bends down and puts a hand in front of the grille*)

GRETA. There should be air blowing through now.

ANNA. There is. (*She straightens, and moves back to Greta*) Then there's . . . (*She consults her book, then her attention returns to the grille*) Do you think they'll know that trick?

GRETA. They might, if there's a professional among them.

ANNA. Yes. Watch for the one who knows about a gentle seepage of truth gas, eh? (*She turns her attention to the book*) The German. Yes. Miss Jane Walters, twenty-five, English. And Miss Louise Delaney, Posford, New Jersey. American. She's thirty.

GRETA. American.

ANNA. Americans *have* been known to spy. (*She shuts the notebook with a snap, and once more betrays her anxiety about the proposed interrogation*) Look, if there's anything you can't handle, let me know. It's in your hands. And so am I, God help me.

GRETA (*moving to the grille*) Shall I start?

ANNA. Yes.

(GRETA *looks* R *along the corridor*)

GRETA. Kovlev?

GUARD (*off*) Ma'am?

GRETA. Send them.

GUARD (*off*) Yes, ma'am.

ANNA. I'll stay until they're all here.

(*Two commands and a clash of gates are heard off*)

GRETA. You'll report to the superintendent, when—when I've finished?

ANNA. Yes. (*She glances along the passage, then returns into the room*) Here they come.

(*The* GUARD *appears and stands* L *of the open grille door, looking down the corridor at the approaching prisoners. When they come in they are tight-lipped, nervous, quiet for the moment. They are dressed in suitable holiday clothes, as though for a hot European summer. They have handbags, cameras, etc.* MRS MARY VICKERS, *a handsome woman of fifty-two, is the quietest dressed. Her blouse is of very high cut.* LOUISE DELANEY, *the American, is quite the most flamboyant, and her camera is obviously very costly.* MISS DORA BYERS, *a hefty, determined dragon of forty-two, is that dominant type of unmarried female who, in a junior school, can well be responsible for half her Head's staffing troubles.* JANE WALTERS, *an infants' teacher of twenty-five, is nervous and near tears.* FRAULEIN EMMA HIPP *is thirty, haughty and contemptuous. They enter and stand in a huddle*)

I suggest you all sit down.

(MARY, DORA *and* JANE *make a slight move to do so.* EMMA *stands firm, and* LOUISE *is truculent*)

LOUISE. For how *long* do we sit down, this time?

(*This remark sparks off the others*)

DORA		Once again, I *demand* to see the British consul!
MARY		(*more quietly*) Certainly.
EMMA	(*together*)	And the German—the *West* German consul.
LOUISE		And baby makes four. (*Questioningly, at Jane*) Or should I say five?

ANNA. You will not be here long.

LOUISE. That eases my mind one hell of a lot.

EMMA. What do you mean by "long"?

ANNA. I should have said that four of you will not be here for long.

DORA. *Four?* But—oh!

ANNA. One of you is a spy.

DORA		How ridiculous!
MARY	(*together*)	One of *us?*
EMMA		Shrecklich!
JANE		Oh, no, no. It's not possible!

LOUISE. You must be right out of your tiny Central European mind!

ANNA (*topping this*) Quiet! Quiet! Once again, I suggest you sit down.

(*They sit:* LOUISE L *of the table,* JANE *down* R *on the seat against the wall,* MARY *above her, with her arm round Jane,* DORA *above* MARY. EMMA HIPP *stands defiantly up* RC. GRETA *moves* LC. ANNA *stands* C)

Section Officer Janek, here, will be in entire charge of the investigation. How long it takes will depend entirely on your co-operation.

DORA. How? What's going to happen?

ANNA. It will be a *total* search.

MARY. What's that?

ANNA. Just what it says. You will be taken to the interrogation room, one at a time, where you will strip under surveillance.

(*There are some gasps of alarm*)

Your clothing will be examined, yourselves X-rayed and checked, every part of your personal possessions will be scrutinized. We know all the tricks.

LOUISE. And then?

ANNA. If you are cleared, you can go.

DORA. Monstrous! I demand to be allowed to telephone the British consul!

LOUISE (*overlapping*) My, this is going to sound good in the New York papers!

JANE (*in tears*) Oh, this is terrible!

EMMA (*overlapping*) You have no right to keep us prisoners like this! I will not answer your questions!

ANNA (*moving up to the grille*) So this is now the responsibility of Section Officer Janek. Remember, this is Cistomek Castle.

LOUISE. We *won't* forget.

ANNA. One part of it is a tourist attraction. The other part is the strongest prison in Europe. There is no escape.

(ANNA *nods to* GRETA, *who salutes.* ANNA *returns the*

salute, then exits, the GUARD *standing aside for her at attention, then taking up position again behind the grille door*)

DORA (*to Greta; nastily*) So we're in *your* hands.

GRETA (*self-possessed*) Entirely.

LOUISE. Your mama must be proud of you.

GRETA (*coolly*) The woman who bore me was a partisan; I never knew her. When we threw the Germans out, I was a baby. I never knew either of my parents.

EMMA (*edgily*) Oh, you threw the Germans out, did you?

GRETA. Yes. (*She takes up a position* L *of the grille door*) Yes. (*Consulting her list*) Fraulein Emma Hipp?

EMMA. Yes.

GRETA. The rest of you just make yourselves as comfortable as possible.

(EMMA *moves to sit*)

No, not you. We'll see you first, I think.

EMMA. I demand to speak to the German consul . . .

GRETA (*snapping*) You don't demand to speak to *anyone!* (*Pointing to the grille door*) Through that door, you, and be *co-operative!*

(EMMA *glares for a moment, then turns to go*)

Stop! (*She whips away Emma's handbag*)

EMMA. What do you think you're . . .

GRETA. I'll take that. It will save time. Yes. All of you—give me your handbags.

(GRETA *goes round taking the women's handbags, to their mixed protests, which overlaps as she reaches them*)

DORA. This is abominable treatment! We ought to break off diplomatic relations with these people!

MARY. This is really inconsiderate. This is ill-treatment!

JANE. Oh, oh dear! Must they? There are only personal things in mine.

LOUISE. Sounds like they read all the best spy scripts.

GRETA (*returning up* LC) Guard, take their cameras!

(*The* GUARD *comes in and begins to take the cameras, moving round as Greta did, so that Louise is reached last*)

MARY. Cameras? Good heavens, what do they think we've got in them?

DORA. Huh! You're welcome to mine, for what good it is!

EMMA. What do they take us for? Can they be serious?

JANE. There's no picture in mine that could do the slightest harm . . .

(*As* LOUISE'S *camera is taken she hollers, topping the others*)

LOUISE. Hey, you, honeybunch, I want a receipt for that! Hey, that's an eight-hundred-dollar Hasselblad you're swinging around there!

GRETA (*snapping*) Miss Delaney, keep calm!

LOUISE. Calm, she says! Just you tell that gun-toting merry peasant to take care of that thing!

GRETA. If you've nothing to hide, you've nothing to fear!

(*There are more gasps of annoyance from all five women*)

(*To the Guard*) Carry on.

(*The* GUARD *exits with the cameras*)

Now, Fraulein Hipp, *if* you please?

(GRETA *waits at the grille door. With a snort,* EMMA *strides out.* GRETA *imperturbably closes the grille door, locks it, then exits* R *after Emma.* LOUISE *rises and goes to to the grille to see as far along the corridor as she can. A door clashes near by.* JANE *dissolves into tears,* MARY *puts an arm round her.* DORA *sits rigidly, an amusing figure of overdetermination, her arms folded, and a glare in her eye*)

DORA. They'll pay for this.

MARY (*to Jane*) Come, dear. It's not so bad. They've not hurt us, and they're not going to.

(LOUISE *moves to the table and leans on it*)

LOUISE. No.

MARY. No. We're all innocent, aren't we?

DORA. Bah!

LOUISE. If any of you gals got a two-way transceiver in her panties, now's the time to ditch it. (*She prowls round, examining the place, working her way towards the lavatory door*)

(JANE *sobs*)

MARY. Come, dear, there's nothing to worry about.

DORA (*scornfully*) *Nothing?*

MARY (*calmly*) They're very security minded.

LOUISE (*reaching the lavatory door and peering through the keyhole*) You said it! (*She tries the handle, then reacts strongly*) They're so goddamned security minded they even locked up the john!

DORA (*starting up*) I don't believe it! (*She crosses to see for herself*) Well!

LOUISE. If they're too damned long searching, I'm going to give their safe and loft squad a case.

MARY. What?

LOUISE. I shall break in!

DORA. *Very* stupid. (*She marches back and sits again as before, rigidly disapproving*) I should have gone to Brighton with Cousin Maud. She said this was foolish. She *said* so!

LOUISE (*trying the lock again*) Hey, you know—I *could* open this.

MARY (*sharply*) No! (*More gently*) No, please. Don't do anything to annoy them.

(LOUISE *shrugs, relaxes, and strolls across to Mary*)

LOUISE. In this concourse of lady teachers, ma'am, I believe you're the only headmistress. That right?

MARY. Yes.

LOUISE. Then I'm well outranked. You're senior officer. But as for annoying them, hell! They're annoying us plenty!

JANE (*very mildly*) I'm sure Mrs Vickers is right.

LOUISE. O.K. (*She sits on the table, swinging her legs*) Any of you girls like a cigarette?

MARY. No handbags.

LOUISE (*wagging a finger; lightly*) Uhuh. (*She puts her hand down the front of her blouse and extracts a small metal case*) See—I'm an addict. Strategic reserve. (*She opens the case*) I guess they're a little sweaty round the filter tip— (*offering the cigarettes*)—but you're very welcome.

MARY (*taking one*) Thank you.

(LOUISE *rises and offers the case to Dora.* DORA *wags her head, purses her lips, and sits as rigidly as before*)

LOUISE (*shrugging*) O.K. So *rule*, Britannia! (*She strikes a match for Mary, lights her own, then waves the case at Jane*) How 'bout you?

JANE. No, thank you.

LOUISE (*replacing the case*) Cheer up, kid. You're taking this much too hard.

JANE. It's all so—so rough.

LOUISE. What's your class age?

JANE (*becoming a little brighter*) Little ones. Fives, sixes.

LOUISE. I bet they just love you. All the patience in the world.

JANE. I try.

LOUISE. Sure you do. Now me, I teach at a mixed high school in Bermondsey. (*She manages the syllables carefully*)

MARY. Comprehensive, you mean.

LOUISE. Yeah. Some of those mophead delinquents comprehend a darn sight too much. You know something? They wolf-whistle me! That never happened in the States. Still, they say travel broadens the mind. (*To Dora*) What's your speciality, Byers? All-in wrestling?

(DORA, *sensitive about her size, snorts and glares.* LOUISE *moves up* C, *slow and stops, peering upwards. She moves another pace and peers again. The others watch her*)

Yeah. There it is. I'm sure.

(MARY *rises and joins Dora*)

What are you talking about?

MARY (*also peering upwards*) It could be.

JANE (*rising and joining Mary*) What?

LOUISE. Your turn, Byers.

DORA. *What?* (*She rises and joins the others* C, *peering upwards with them*)

LOUISE. Everything we say is being taken down, and may be used you-know-how.

(*For a moment, while* DORA, JANE *and* LOUISE *peer upwards,* MARY *moves slightly* R *and catches sight of the grille under the seat. She gives a little start and, unseen by the others and covered by* JANE'S *and* DORA'S *following remarks, takes a step forward to look harder. She seems to recognize what the grille is, then rejoins the others*)

DORA. A microphone!

JANE. Oh, no! Is it, really?

LOUISE. Wouldn't you say so, Mrs Vickers?

MARY (*moving back quickly*) Yes. Yes, it could be.

DORA. Monstrous!

JANE. How could they?

LOUISE. They could and they do. I wouldn't be surprised if there was a closed-circuit TV camera somewhere. But where?

(*The group separates.* LOUISE *prowls around* L)

JANE. Oh, it makes me feel all—all exposed!

LOUISE. That's nothing to the exposure you'll get later, sweetheart.

DORA. Vulgar! (*She marches back to her place and sits*)

MARY (*signalling to Louise*) Psst!

LOUISE. Huh?

(MARY *moves down* R *and beckons* LOUISE *to follow her.* MARY *points under the seat.* DORA *and* JANE *listen.* MARY *takes off her silk scarf and, with the others watching, stuffs it carefully into the grille. Then she straightens*)

What gives?

MARY (*quietly*) I think what you saw up there—

(*pointing to the ceiling*)—is a dummy. I think that the real mike's in *there!*

(LOUISE *looks for a moment, then chuckles.* MARY *chuckles also*)

LOUISE (*to Dora*) Come on, Byers, bust a stay with us. (*To Mary; more confidentially*) Hey, that was smart. How long have you been working for the C.I.A.? Or what do you British call it?

MARY. I've no idea. I just didn't like the idea of being spied on—you see.

LOUISE (*thinking it hilarious*) Ha! I bet the recording boys are going crazy.

(*The door clashes off, and footsteps are heard*)

Hey, back to places.

(*They all sit as before.* GRETA *comes along the corridor;* EMMA, *angry and dishevelled, follows. Least comes the* GUARD *with Emma's camera and handbag.* GRETA *unlocks the grille door and stands aside.* EMMA *snatches her belongings and enters. The* GUARD *and* GRETA *remain outside.* EMMA *stands* LC)

GRETA. Miss Byers.

(*After a moment of silence* DORA *rises, a bit scared, and walks to the grille. She passes through, the* GUARD *shuts the door and locks it.* EMMA *begins to arrange herself.* DORA *starts to go off down th corridor*)

LOUISE. Show 'em a full Nelson, Britannia!

(DORA *glares and exits, followed by* GRETA *and the* GUARD. EMMA, *tidying herself, is so angry that she cannot speak coherently for a moment. She tries to tug herself straight and grunts with rage*)

LOUISE. Can I help?
EMMA. Let me alone!
LOUISE. Well, if you feel like that . . .
EMMA (*trying to keep herself from weeping*) The insulting, probing swine! (*She moves down* LC)

JANE. Was it—bad?

MARY. Hands above head holding grips, feet astride?

EMMA (*still struggling*) Yes. (*Realizing, she stops*) How did you know?

MARY. Standard German procedure, during the war. But they didn't always have women interrogated *by* women.

(EMMA *glares and* JANE *looks fearful*)

LOUISE (*softly*) Oh, boy. *Touchée!*

(EMMA *glares enquiringly*)

MARY. I read about it.

(EMMA *snorts*)

JANE. Does that—that young one do it—the searching, I mean?

EMMA (*viciously*) No. But she watches. *How* she watches! (*She finishes with her clothes and tries, without a mirror, to do her hair. She remains angry*)

MARY. Do they—does she have dossiers for us?

LOUISE (*incredulously*) What? Personal files for all of us?

EMMA (*still struggling with her hair*) No, she doesn't seem to. But she did make a phone call to some document registry, I think it was. And she has a photograph.

JANE. What photograph?

EMMA. I didn't see. (*She sighs with exasperation, then moves in a pace*) Who is it?

(*There is an uncomprehending silence*)

MARY. Who is *what?*

EMMA. The spy, of course.

LOUISE. *You* think it's one of us?

EMMA. Certainly. And it would be easier for us all if the one who it is owned up.

JANE. Oh!

MARY. It might be easier for four of us, I agree, *if* one of us is indeed a spy.

LOUISE. If I were the one . . .

EMMA. Yes?

LOUISE. I wouldn't burn for anybody. I'd sweat it out.

EMMA. One of us is lying.

MARY (*to Louise*) It does *look* as though someone's lying.

LOUISE. Someone. O.K. But don't look at me. I'm just an exchange teacher who thought she'd do Europe and who got done *by* Europe instead!

EMMA. Huh. You Americans, you are not serious.

LOUISE. Oh. And you are?

EMMA. We Europeans understand this—this sort of situation better, I think.

LOUISE. Oh. Yes. I see. Some of your Europeans are specialists, aren't you? (*Her voice rises*)

(MARY *rises and moves above the table*)

My papa met some when he escaped from prison camp— they wore black S.S. uniforms!

JANE. Oh, don't quarrel, please.

MARY. She's right. It's undignified, you know. Unprofessional.

(*There is a pause.* MARY *sits* R *of the table*)

JANE. But—you know—one of us *could* be.

EMMA. Yes. (*She sits on the bench* L)

MARY. How do you combine teaching with spying?

JANE. Well—I don't think you have to. One of us could be a sleeper.

LOUISE. *That's* possible.

EMMA. What do you mean?

JANE. They train someone, put them in a certain place or position and they don't do any spying for years and years. Then the spy does one job, and after it he— she . . .

LOUISE. Goes back to sleep? (*She shrugs*) Sounds like real TV spy stuff to me. Maybe the fiction's really fact. What do you say, *Untergruppenfuhrerein* Hipp?

(EMMA *glares at her*)

O.K. I'll promote you. *Obergruppenfuhrerein* Hipp.

(EMMA *rises and moves* L *of Louise*)

EMMA. Why do you hate the Germans?

LOUISE. Looking for love, sweetheart? Not from me. My papa was rescued soon after those S.S. men finished with him. He spent about ten years in a wheel-chair.

JANE (*scared*) And now?

LOUISE. No *now*. He took fifty Nembutal tablets one night—and that was that. (*She looks at Emma*)

JANE (*softly*) Oh.

MARY. I'm sorry.

EMMA. Don't you look at me! I was too young for any of that. I wasn't even in the Hitler Youth!

LOUISE. What a thrill you missed!

(EMMA *takes a swipe at Louise.* JANE *and* MARY *start to their feet with cries of alarm.* LOUISE *slips from her chair, sidesteps, grabs Emma's arm and twists it.* EMMA, *with a howl of rage, measures her length on the floor down* LC. LOUISE *takes it easily*)

Watch it, dearie. I have other hobbies besides photography.

(EMMA *gets up, scowling, and dusts herself.* MARY *and* JANE *sit in their original places on the seat* R. LOUISE *moves* R *of the table and sits.* EMMA *sits* L *of the table*)

(*To Emma*) Sorry. But you asked for it. (*Turning to the other two*) That was *civil* experience in that throw, not military, if anyone's thinking things.

MARY. I suppose I'm the only one here with military experience.

LOUISE. What kind?

MARY. A.T.S. I drove lorries in the war.

JANE. I'm sure that wouldn't—er—*count* . . .

MARY (*smiling*) Against me?

EMMA. With these people, how do you tell?

(*There is the clash of an iron grille off* R)

LOUISE. My, they're speedy!

(DORA BYERS *is escorted back by* GRETA *and the* GUARD. *The same procedure is adopted as before when Emma returned.* GRETA *this time carries a file.* DORA *is furious and dishevelled as she stumbles in, and carries her blouse over her arm. She moves down* LC, *and we are surprised to see that her slip is bright red.* GRETA *stands* C, *beautifully unruffled, impassive*)

GRETA (*calling the next name*) Miss Walters, please.

(JANE *rises nervously*)

MARY. There's nothing to worry about, dear.

(JANE *passes through the grille*)

GRETA. Nothing to worry about, if you are innocent.

(*The gate is locked and* JANE, GRETA *and the* GUARD *exit.* DORA, *trembling with anger and fear, tries to tidy herself up*)

DORA (*bursting out*) The beasts! The prying, shoving, *indecent* beasts!

(EMMA *rises, moves to the seat* L *and sits apart.* MARY *and* LOUISE *rise and go to Dora.* DORA *sobs unrestrainedly*)

MARY (*standing* R *of Dora*) It's an investigation, you know. The standard procedure.

DORA (*still tearful*) Whose side are you on?

LOUISE (*moving* L *of Dora*) Dammit, Byers, be your age!

DORA. My hair, my ears, everything. I've never been so—so *insulted!* I—I never dreamed they . . .

LOUISE. Just what was it they did that set you off?

DORA. I think it was—my toenails.

MARY. Toenails?

DORA. They—they scraped under every one! Why in heaven's name did they have to do that? (*She finishes tidying herself*)

MARY (*moving round* R *of the table and facing the others*) Now look, there's no point in recriminating. We are five teachers east of what used to be called the Iron Curtain . . .

DORA		*Used* to be? I've never been so
	(*together*)	insulted . . .
EMMA		It's still there!

MARY. These people are in pretty good shape socially, economically, now. Many of them want closer ties with the West. Why should we want to scare them off with spies?

EMMA. We?

MARY. Western governments.

EMMA. Huh!

LOUISE. Can't say I feel they've been very encouraging to *us*.

MARY. But that's taking it personally. (*She sits down* R)

LOUISE (*moving above the table and sitting* R) How the hell else am I to take it? This sweetness and light kick seems overworked to me, right now, and I've not yet been in for treatment. No doubt I'll emerge a little ruffled.

DORA. Ruffled!

LOUISE. Butch Britannia over there'll be taking this out of her suffering kids for the next five years.

DORA. Oh! (*She sits* L *of the table*)

MARY. These people, in this country, are ready now to come a little closer to the Western way of thinking. They're nervous, though, they're trapped between two fires. They remember how, at the end of the war, British soldiers were ordered to fire on their partisans.

EMMA. How do you know all this?

MARY. Reading. Good Sunday newspapers, plus history books.

LOUISE. So what's this leading up to?

MARY (*rising; with a short sigh and an appraisal of each one present*) This. Can we assume that no one of us is a spy?

DORA		(*angrily*) Of course!
LOUISE	(*together*)	The C.I.A. never heard of me!
EMMA		I do not spy!

MARY. And I don't, either.

LOUISE. How about babykins, down to the buff in that interrogation room right now?

DORA. No!

MARY. She's a good teacher, I'm sure. But she doesn't have the qualities—for the other job.

LOUISE. So what are you saying?

MARY. That one of us *could* be a *provocateur*.

(*There is a shocked silence*)

DORA. No!

LOUISE. One of *us*, working for *them?*

EMMA. How do you distinguish between *us* and *them?*

DORA (*rising*) Are you suggesting that all this dreadful interrogation business was a blind? That someone is trying to trap us?

LOUISE (*remembering something*) Just a minute. (*She crosses below Mary to the plugged grille down* R) You sure this mike is muffled, O.K.?

MARY. Yes. Isn't it?

LOUISE. I think so. (*She moves back to her seat*) You figure that one of us was actually planted in England and followed us out here to—to . . .

MARY. Yes.

DORA. To—to spy on the spy?

MARY. Yes.

(*There is a silence.* EMMA *rises and moves in.* **They all stare at one another**)

EMMA. Who?

LOUISE. Sister, you got me nervous again.

DORA (*working things out, and not liking what she finds*) You mean that one of us went up there to *report*, *not* to be interrogated?

MARY. Went up there, *is* up there, or is *going* up there.

(*The others take this in*)

LOUISE. You're including *me?*

EMMA. She's including *herself*.

MARY. Certainly.

DORA. Mrs Vickers, that's stupid.

MARY (*to Dora*) You might think it is, but how do they know it isn't?

DORA. Pah!

MARY. How does any of us know that it isn't one of the other four?

LOUISE. I get the point. We don't.

MARY. Exactly.

DORA. Somebody's a very good liar.

MARY. Lying is a basic requisite.

(*Now they are all suspicious of one another. They separate.* EMMA *sits* L *again,* DORA *moves up* LC. MARY *sits down* R. LOUISE *lights a cigarette*)

EMMA. This now becomes unpleasant.

DORA. Huh! It was never anything else!

LOUISE (*softly but fiercely*) If one of the five has got us into this mess, I'll break her damned neck.

EMMA. Hah. I'm glad I am innocent.

LOUISE. Innocent?

EMMA. Yes.

LOUISE. What do you mean, Fraulein Hipp, honey, is that you're not a spy.

EMMA. That is what I said.

LOUISE. Not in my language it isn't. You work it out.

(*There is the clash of a door off* R)

MARY. *That* was quick.

LOUISE. Maybe too quick.

(*The* GUARD *and* GRETA *appear, the latter carrying the same file as before, with another piece of white board, evidently a photograph, which does not fit the file, sticking out from it. She also has some other papers. The* GUARD *opens the door,* GRETA *stands just outside and beckons to those within*)

GRETA. Come along.

(*There is a moment's hesitation. They look at one another: then comes the outburst. Everyone rises and moves up towards the grille,* MARY *and* LOUISE R *of it,* DORA *and* EMMA L)

MARY		Jane! She's not come back? Where's Jane?
LOUISE		Hey—where's that infant child teacher got to?
EMMA	(*together*)	So—the mild and gentle one has not returned!
DORA		Oh no, no! It could never be Jane! There must be some mistake.

(GRETA *is momentarily taken aback, then she tops the outburst before they have finished*)

GRETA. Quiet, please. *Quiet!* (*She comes forward into the cell. There is some strain and anxiety in her manner, which she fights*) There was no sense in bringing her down again.

LOUISE. What's going on?

GRETA. Miss Byers, Fraulein Hipp, Miss Delaney, you may go upstairs, where your personal belongings will be restored to you.

(*All except* MARY *give vent to cries of relief*)

LOUISE		Well, so they finally made up their minds!
DORA	(*together*)	I should think so, treating us like this.
EMMA		This will bring some publicity, I assure you!

(*Then they realize that Mary Vickers's name has not been mentioned. They look at Mary*)

LOUISE. Hey, did you say Mrs Vickers's name?

GRETA. No. I—want to have a talk with her.

EMMA. You are going to interrogate her here?

GRETA. A talk, I said.

(*They look at one another*)

EMMA. Is she not in the same position as the rest of us? (*She takes a step towards Greta*) Well—what is the difference?

GRETA. It need not concern you at all.

LOUISE. Now wait a minute, my little section officer . . .

GRETA (*sharply*) Miss Delaney! Throwing your weight about will not do the slightest good. You have been told to go upstairs. Do you want to be driven to freedom?

DORA (*suddenly becoming brave*) I demand to know what is happening!

GRETA. Demand?

DORA. Jane Walters upstairs—and—and Mrs Vickers

down here—*what is going on? (An hysterical note creeps in)*
I demand to know! *(She ends on a scream)*

(GRETA, *quite calmly, slaps Dora's face twice, hard.*
DORA *moans.* LOUISE *moves to her, and supports her,*
together with EMMA)

LOUISE. Did you have to?
GRETA. Yes. Now, outside, please.

(DORA *sobs and exits, supported by* EMMA *and* LOUISE.
They stop outside the grille, and look back at Mary)

(Coldly) Don't miss your bus, ladies.

(DORA, EMMA *and* LOUISE *exit down the corridor, fol-*
lowed by the GUARD)

(Turning to Mary) Please sit down, Mrs Vickers.
MARY. So I *am* to be interrogated.
GRETA. Separately. And differently. Please sit down.

(MARY *sits* R *of the table.* GRETA *sits* L *of it, arranging*
files and papers, deliberately taking her time. It is as though
she is determined to summon all her reserves)

MARY. I should like to catch the bus, too.
GRETA *(after a pause, without lifting her eyes)* No doubt.
MARY. It leaves at five.
GRETA *(still looking down at her papers)* I know.
MARY. If you want me to strip . . .
GRETA. Did I say so?
MARY. Why do you choose to treat me differently?

(GRETA *looks up sharply, and slams the table)*

GRETA *(snapping)* *I* am responsible for this investiga-
tion! Wholly! *(More quietly)* It's very simple, Mrs
Vickers. I ask, you answer. Is that clear?
MARY. Quite clear.
GRETA. Just do as you're asked, and we'll manage
without threats, or guards, or the indignities which the
others suffered. All right?
MARY. Yes.
GRETA *(settling down to the documents, and the routine)*

You are Mary Natalie Vickers, of forty-five Ormond Road, Catford, London.

MARY. Yes.

GRETA. You are fifty-two years old, and a teacher.

MARY. Yes.

GRETA. A headmistress.

MARY. Yes.

GRETA. And your subjects, when you taught classes, were languages.

MARY. Yes. (*Puzzled*) You have that down there—without questioning me? How does that happen? Did Jane Walters tell you that I . . .

GRETA. *I* do the questioning. French, German and Spanish?

MARY. Yes.

GRETA. Then you do not speak Helleno-Croat, the language of this country?

MARY. Just a few words I learned before I came here. I have done some Greek, and there are strong affinities . . .

GRETA. Yes, yes, I know. This is your first visit to this country, then?

MARY. Yes.

GRETA. You know nothing of its customs or history?

MARY. Only what one may commonly read.

GRETA. Do you know anything about the German occupation?

MARY. Of course.

GRETA. What do you know?

MARY. All English people know of your heroism, during the occupation.

GRETA. All?

MARY. There is sympathy, in England, for your country.

GRETA. How?

MARY. For what it did during the war, and for the—er—present difficulties it faces.

GRETA. Difficulties?

MARY. Dilemma, perhaps. Its need to be independently Communist.

GRETA. And this is widely discussed in England?

MARY. Yes.

GRETA. And you remain firm in your statement that this is your first visit?

MARY. I do.

GRETA. What family do you have?

MARY. My husband left me.

GRETA. But—you keep his name?

MARY. I find it convenient.

GRETA. Children?

MARY (*after a fractional hesitation*) No.

GRETA (*with a long, searching look*) You have had no children?

MARY. No.

GRETA. A doctor could soon check that.

MARY. Certainly. Section officer, what *is* the point of this? You can verify my identity with the British consul if you wish . . .

GRETA. We'll do this my way, please. (*She gives Mary a long stare, very gravely, then rises and, during the following speeches, walks around* C *and* LC) Your *first* visit.

MARY. Yes.

GRETA. As Mrs Mary Vickers.

MARY. I don't understand.

GRETA. What was your name before you were married?

MARY. Lucas.

GRETA (*facing away from her*) Not—Lucasza?

(MARY *starts slightly, but answers steadily*)

MARY. What was that?

GRETA (*articulating distinctly*) Lucasza.

MARY. The name means nothing to me. My name was Lucas.

GRETA. H'm. (*She returns* L *of the table and, standing, picks up a document from the file and reads*) "Maria Nerid Lucasza. Born Porovgrad June eighth, nineteen-thirteen. Daughter of Julian Erik Lucasza, schoolmaster, and Maria Lucasza. Won an Estervan scholarship to Oxford, first-class honours, taught in England until the outbreak of war." (*She throws down the paper*) And this is not you?

MARY. No.

GRETA. There is no connection between Maria Nerid Lucasza and Mary Natalie Vickers?

MARY (*steadily*) If you want some, you will have to manufacture it.

GRETA (*snapping*) I don't *need* to manufacture evidence! (*More calmly*) I am highly regarded in the service.

MARY. The secret police?

GRETA. The prison section of the *ordinary* police! That is the only kind we have! Now! (*She walks away a couple of steps, then turns and raps out a question*) Can you remember the drill for fitting a British Irvine parachute harness?

MARY. What? (*Laughing*) Really, section officer, I came here from Athens, by coach.

GRETA. This time you did, *this* time!

MARY. This is the first . . .

GRETA. What were your intentions on *this* occasion, Maria Lucasza?

MARY. Why, to see the sights. The Darina woods, the twin cathedrals, to spend a few days in Porovgrad—the itinerary approved by your tourist board, which *does* include Cistomek castle. (*With a snap*) And my name is Mary Vickers.

GRETA. Formerly Lucas.

MARY. Yes.

GRETA. Who has never been here before, eh?

MARY. Never.

(*From this point on it gradually becomes clear that* GRETA *for all her self-control, is suffering from considerable strain. It is as though she were conducting the interrogation against her own inclinations. She loses her ease, becomes tense, and more and more refers to that photograph which does not seem to fit into the dossier on account of its size*)

GRETA (*pacing*) You mean—you have never been *here*.

MARY. I don't understand.

GRETA. Perhaps you know the Robanka Mountains better?

MARY. The Robanka Mountains *are* on the itinerary, but we were intending to visit them next week, when . . .

GRETA (*snapping, almost in a shout*) I know! (*She returns to the table and consults the dossier again, in particular the big old photograph*) You know that there are parts of the Robanka Mountains which are very special?

MARY. Oh, yes. We saw pictures of the ceremonies on television.

GRETA. Holy ground. Parts of the mountains, along with the partisan stronghold, the hill of caves, have been called holy ground. Holy. It appeals to some people, no doubt.

MARY. I don't understand.

GRETA We could have done with God's help *then*, I believe, not with the so-called hallowing twenty years later.

MARY. But you're not old enough to remember that.

GRETA. Of course not. I was less than a year old. (*She moves above the table, close to Mary, and speaks very quietly*) Did you ever read about the partisans' last stand, there?

MARY (*quietly*) Yes, I—read about it. The burning of the three villages, down in the valley . . .

GRETA (*starting quietly, but working up to a climax as she goes on*) Almost everyone in those three villages, Indiska, Badec and Kovad, was murdered. I—*I* am the sole survivor of Kovad, the only living one. The others, three-hundred and twenty-five of them, were dragged from their homes, locked in the village church, which was then set on fire. The S.S. men shot the few who managed to get out; the rest died in the flames. Their screams still echo round the valley; even for *God* they will not be quiet.

MARY. I read about that, too.

GRETA (*reaching a passionate, bitter climax*) You only *read* about it!

MARY. Yes. I read about it.

(*As GRETA becomes more and more tense, MARY seems to go in the opposite direction, to become quieter and more relaxed. As* MARY *utterly controls herself and shows no strain,* GRETA *becomes less and less successful at hiding the mounting tension. She walks about, turning and "throwing" her remarks and questions, while* MARY *sits quietly at the table*)

GRETA. Where do you imagine the microphone is, in this place?

MARY. I think you heard.

GRETA. You feel sure of that?

MARY. Not completely. But a hidden microphone is standard procedure, isn't it?

GRETA. Yes. Along with the hidden cameras in the interrogation room and the dressing room.

MARY. You find them necessary?

GRETA. Yes. We trust in our president, and keep our powder dry.

MARY. That isn't the way I first heard that quotation.

GRETA. It's the way you hear it now. (*Moving up* C *and pointing above her head*) You *know* about microphones.

MARY. You heard what I know, perhaps.

GRETA. Perhaps I didn't hear *all* you know. When the American pointed out the microphone up there, you said you thought that one was a decoy, and that the real microphone was hidden somewhere else.

MARY. Was I wrong?

GRETA. Maria Lucasza, you are very smart. All the conversation in this room was recorded with complete clarity. How do you account for that?

MARY. I don't account for it. I could have been wrong. Just as you are wrong when you call me Maria Lucasza.

GRETA. You pronounced the name very well.

MARY. I told you. I have an ear for languages.

GRETA. And a talent for strange mistakes. Well, we can all make mistakes. can't we? (*She picks up the large photograph and studies it*)

MARY. You interrogate me here——

(GRETA *looks up at her, the hand gripping the photograph shakes a little*)

—and all the others were interrogated in the—the proper place. Why?

GRETA. Save your questions. Mine are the ones that count. (*She places the photograph in front of Mary*) Look. Go on, take it.

(MARY *picks up the photograph, remaining very calm*)

What do you see?

MARY. It seems to be a group of young people, roughly clad, standing on a mountainside. They are armed with rifles and Schmeissers. Partisans?

GRETA. Partisans. (*Moving above the table, closer to Mary*) You see the young man and woman on the left? At the back?

MARY. Yes.

GRETA. Their name was Janek.

MARY. The same as yours?

GRETA. Yes. My father and mother.

(MARY *looks surprised*)

Yes, married partisans. They had a child.

MARY. With them? In those conditions?

GRETA. She had her baby one night in the village of Kovad. She left it there, with a family. Good people. The Janeks were experts at wrecking and demolitions. Nothing was allowed to intefere with that.

MARY. It seems—brave.

GRETA. It was. But let me tell you more about the Janeks. She had been born here, in this country, but, when the Germans invaded, she parachuted down from Britain, with a long-range radio kit, and stayed with it, sending messages to London, asking for supplies, keeping the British government informed.

MARY. If you'd explain what this has to do with me . . .

GRETA (*shouting*) Listen! (*More quietly*) On one occasion, it is recorded, she ran two miles through scrub and mountain brush, lugging her radio kit, with the Germans after her. She was wounded; a bullet ripped across here (*she runs a finger across her collar-bone*)——

(MARY, *almost involuntarily, puts her hand up to her high-necked blouse*)

—and laid her collar-bone bare.

(*Now there is anxiety on* MARY'S *face, too, but* GRETA *suffers the stronger emotion by far. She stares at Mary, then moves below the table to the grille down* R *and takes the scarf from it. As she is bending down, she sees something clipped magnetically to one of the metal bench supports. It is a small black object, the size of a cigarette lighter. She looks at it, examines it, and is greatly shocked and disturbed. She attempts to recover her composure, and pockets the metal object as she stands. Then she walks carefully above the table to* L *of it, faces Mary, and tosses the scarf on to the table*)

Yours?

MARY. Yes.

GRETA. And what was it doing there?

MARY. You know.

GRETA. Tell me.

MARY. To muffle the microphone.

GRETA. No! You knew where the microphone was, up there in the ceiling! You stuffed the scarf in the grill because that was where the real danger was. You knew that from that grille seeps a gas derived from scopalomine—the truth drug! If you hadn't done that, and made the excuse when you did it, you would have been speaking the truth—*all* of you! (*She shakes a little*)

MARY (*pointing to the ceiling*) I thought the real microphone was there.

GRETA (*quietly*) And you are *not* a resurrected British agent, are you?

(*It becomes really quiet now. The offstage noises are softened too, as though the whole prison were listening*)

MARY. You know who I am.

GRETA. Yes. Yes—I know you; I know who you are. (*She shuts the dossier with a snap, moves to the grille door, opens it, and stands aside*)

MARY (*rising and moving up towards the door a little*) I am to go?

GRETA. Yes. Collect your belongings upstairs. You can still—catch the bus. (*She trembles*)

(MARY *moves to the door and faces Greta, wonder, alarm and incredulity on her face*)

MARY. There is something about your eyes . . .
GRETA (*snapping*) Go, at once!

(MARY *stares at Greta in concern, then exits quickly. The prison noises go on.* GRETA *goes to the wall telephone, is on the point of using it, then decides against it. She comes down to the table, throws down the file, and picks up the photograph she had shown to Mary. Staring at it, she sinks into the chair* L *of the table*)

(*With a groan*) It must be! (*She takes the miniature camera from her pocket and looks at it*) It's certain, certain! (*She covers her face with her hands*)

(*There is a pause, then* ANNA KRISNOV *comes along the corridor and enters briskly*)

ANNA (*moving down* R *of the table*) Cleared it all up then, Section Officer? (*She notices Greta's condition, and her manner changes. With a noticeable hardening in her attitude*) What's the matter, girl?

(GRETA *looks up at Anna, very distressed*)

(*Picking up the photograph*) This isn't from an official file, is it?
GRETA. No, it isn't. It's mine.

(ANNA *stares at her, then grabs the micro-camera*)

ANNA. You found *this* camera?

(GRETA *nods*)

Good work. I thought you'd make out. I did wonder about your toughness, I admit, but this seems to have settled it. I was wrong. (*She tosses the micro-camera in her hand, then goes to the wall phone. With one hand on the receiver, she turns*) Where did you put her?

(GRETA *does not reply*)

(*Moving above the table*) Janek?

GRETA (*weeping*) I let her go.

ANNA (*unable to take it in*) You *what?* (*She stares*) Good God! (*She hastens to the phone, grabs the receiver, and stabs a button*)

(GRETA *rises and follows Anna, standing close to her*)

(*Into the receiver*) Guardroom! Guardroom, *at once!* (*She turns and snarls at Greta*) I must—I must have been off my head! Where the hell was my judgement! (*Into the receiver*) Come on, damn you, answer!

GRETA. She—she was my mother!

ANNA (*into the receiver*) Guardroom! Assistant Super-intendent here! There's a woman coming through—middle-aged, grey-haired, English. She should still be in the inner keep. Take her and put her in a cell! Got that? Right! (*She replaces the receiver*)

(GRETA *turns and collapses on to the chair* L *of the table*)

GRETA. I couldn't do it! She was so brave, once. And to find that she—she—oh, I couldn't. Don't you *understand?*

ANNA. Understand? You're the one who doesn't understand! You stupid, gutless, witless ninny, I knew who she was before she ever set a foot in Cistomek!

GRETA. What?

ANNA. Yes! I knew! Intelligence knew twenty-four hours ago! But, like a damned fool, I thought you were good enough for this job, so I persuaded Mischek to let you do the interrogation; I felt sure you'd stand up to it. I swore to Mischek that it was safe to let this idea go through, and you've let me down! (*She grabs Greta roughly under the chin and holds up her sorrowing face*) Now you listen to me, my girl—I'm not sacrificing my pension and rank for you! So, when that woman is brought down here again, and stripped and locked up, you will then write a convincing report which details how you discovered her, and the action you took. Don't worry about the guardroom log—I'll fix that.

GRETA. No—oh, I couldn't . . . !

(ANNA *moves up to the grille and stands there, raging and resolute*)

ANNA (*jerking a thumb at the door*) Move!

(GRETA *rises and moves brokenly towards the exit. When she reaches it she stops and faces Anna*)

(*Without a scrap of pity on her face*) This is the last time I risk anything for anyone. Make one false step, and next week I'll have you back here as general-duty cleaner. Understand?

(GRETA *nods, then goes.* ANNA *comes back to the table and picks up the file and the photograph. She stares angrily at the latter*)

Trust. It doesn't mean a damn thing!

ANNA *slaps the photographs back into the file, and goes out briskly. For a moment the stage remains empty. The prison noises go on, as—*

the CURTAIN *falls*

FURNITURE AND PROPERTY LIST

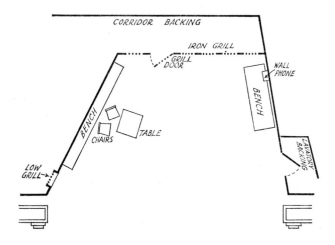

On stage: Bench (clamped to wall R) *On it:* duster. *Attached
to metal support out of sight:* miniature camera
Bench (against wall L)
Table (against bench R)
2 wooden chairs (against bench R)
On wall up L: wall telephone

Off stage: Broom, mop, bucket, brush and pan (JOVANKA)
Sub-machine-gun (GUARD)
Bunch of keys (GRETA)
File, photograph and papers (GRETA)

Personal: JOVANKA: cigarette
ANNA: notebook
MARY: handbag, camera

LOUISE: handbag, camera, cigarette case, matches
DORA: handbag, camera
EMMA: handbag, camera
GRETA: list

MADE AND PRINTED IN GREAT BRITAIN BY
LATIMER TREND AND CO. LTD, PLYMOUTH
MADE IN ENGLAND

LIGHTING PLOT

Property fittings required: guarded wall light in corridor
 Interior. A prison cell and corridor
  THE APPARENT SOURCES OF LIGHT are a window high in
   the "fourth wall" and a wall light in the corridor
  THE MAIN ACTING AREAS are down R, RC, up and down C,
   up and down LC

To open: Effect of dull daylight. Corridor light on
No cues

EFFECTS PLOT

Cue 1	At opening	(Page 1)
	Prison noises, clang of gates, voices distorted by loudspeakers, occasional bursts of martial music. Continue at discretion throughout	
Cue 2	JOVANKA exits into lavatory	(Page 2)
	Cistern flushes	
Cue 3	GRETA: ". . . at your word, ma'am."	(Page 4)
	Telephone buzzes	
Cue 4	GRETA: ". . . British agent, are you?"	(Page 30)
	Prison noises quieten down	
Cue 5	At end of play	(Page 33)
	Prison noises grow louder	